4

14

22

26

30

M	T	W	T	F	S	S
		1	2	3	4	5
6	7	8	9	10	11	12
13	14	15	16	17	18	19
20	21	22	23	24	25	26
27	28	29	30	31		

A ➡ B   A ⇄ B

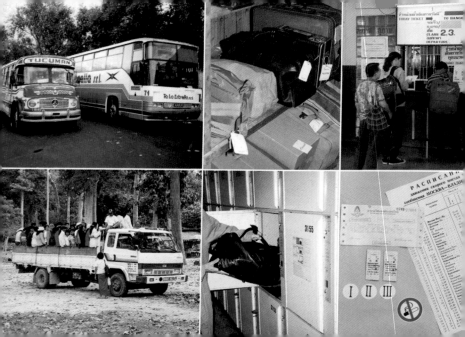

Ag Au

For special sights of interest use postcards or your guidebook's photos.

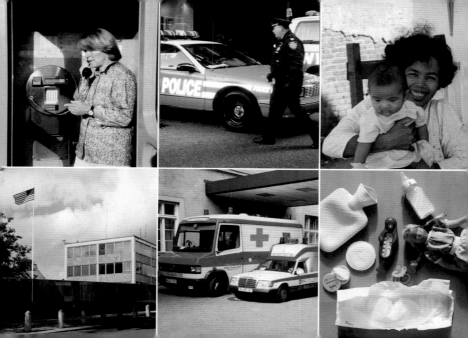

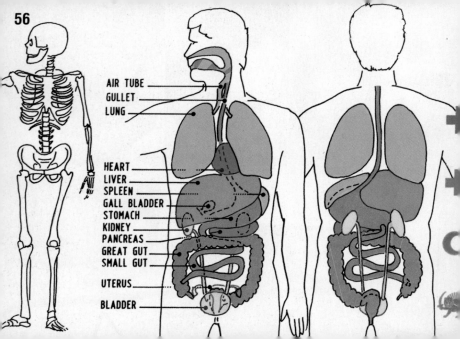

56

AIR TUBE
GULLET
LUNG

HEART
LIVER
SPLEEN
GALL BLADDER
STOMACH
KIDNEY
PANCREAS
GREAT GUT
SMALL GUT

UTERUS

BLADDER

WORLD

AFRICA

OCEAN

ATLANTIC OCEAN

INDIAN OCEAN

Mer Méditerranée

Red Sea

Gulf of Guinea

Countries and regions:

UZBEKISTAN · TURKMENISTAN · IRAN · GEORGIA · SSAKH · ARMENIA · IRAQ · UNITED ARAB EMIRATES · UMAN · AL-ARABIYA AS-SAUDIYA · AL-YAMAN · SOOMAALIYA · ITYOPYA · DJIBOUTI · SOURIYA · LEBANON · ISRAEL · URDUNN E-Kahra/JORDAN · TÜRKIYE · ELLAS · ITALIA · PORTUGAL · ESPAÑA · MAROC · AL-MAGHRIB · ALGÉRIE · TUNÍSIA · LIBIYA · MISR EGYPT · AS-SUDAN · TCHAD · NIGER · MALI · MAWRITANIYAH · SAHARA · SENEGAL · GAMBIA · GUINEE BISSAU · GUINEE · SIERRA LEONE · LIBERIA · CÔTE D'IVOIRE · BURKINA FASO · GHANA · TOGO · DAHOMEY · NIGERIA · CAMEROUN · CENTRAFRICAINE RÉP. · GUINEA EQUATORIAL · SÃO TOMÉ E PRÍNCIPE · GABON · CONGO · RÉP. DU CONGO · UGANDA · KENYA · TANZANIA · RWANDA · BURUNDI · ANGOLA · ZAMBIA · MALAWI · MOÇAMBIQUE · ZIMBABWE · BOTSWANA · NAMIBIA · REP. OF SOUTH AFRICA · LESOTHO · NGWANE · MADAGASIKARA

St. Helena (U.K.) · Ascension (U.K.) · Tristan da Cunha (U.K.) · Google-Is. (U.K.) · Islas Canarias (esp.) · Azore · Madeira (port.) · Seychelles (U.K.) · Pr.-Edward-Is. · Comores · Réunion (fr.)

Tropic of Cancer · Tropic of Capricorn · Equator

Cape of Good Hope · Cape Town

0   500   1000   1500 km

Northpole (geogr.)

ROSSIJA

ARCTIC OCEAN

ISLAND
Reykjavik

Greenland (dan., auton.)

Northpole (magn.)

Baffin Bay

Baffin Island

Davis Str.

Hudson Bay

Queen Elizabeth Islands

Victoria Island

Beaufort Sea

Alaska

Gulf of Alaska

PACIFIC OCEAN

CANADA

U.S.A.

Gulf of Mexico

MEXICO

GUATEMALA
BELIZE
HONDURAS
EL SALVADOR
NICARAGUA
COSTA RICA
PANAMA

BAHAMAS
CUBA
JAMAICA
HAITI
DOM. REP.
Antillas Mayores
Caribbean Sea

ATLANTIC OCEAN

Bermuda (U.K.)

Tropic of Cancer

NORTH AMERICA

0   500   1000   1500 km

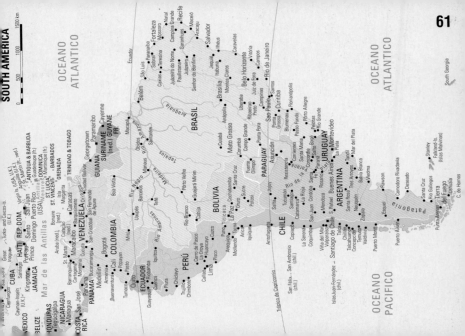